THAT'S OUR NURSE!

The author and photographer would like to thank all the many teachers, administrators, other faculty members, children and parents at P.S. 87, Manhattan, for their inspiring school and generous cooperation in the making of this book. Special thanks to Stephen Brown for all his wonderful help and support in the preparation of the manuscript.

Library of Congress Cataloging-in-Publication Data
Morris, Ann, 1930-
That's our nurse!/Ann Morris; photographs and illustrations by Peter Linenthal.
p. cm.—(That's our school)
Summary: Introduces Mrs. Geary, an elementary school nurse, describing what she does during the school day and how she interacts with other staff and students.
ISBN 0-7613-2402-X (lib. bdg.)
1. School nursing—Juvenile literature.   [1. School nursing.
2. Nurses.   3. Occupations.]   I. Linenthal, Peter, ill.   II. Title.
RJ247.M67   2003
371.7'12—dc21   2002155131

The Millbrook Press, Inc.
2 Old New Milford Road
Brookfield, Connecticut 06804
www.millbrookpress.com

THAT'S OUR NURSE!

Ann Morris

Photographs and Illustrations
by Peter Linenthal

The Millbrook Press / Brookfield, Connecticut

Mrs. Geary is the nurse in our school. She takes good care of us if we're sick. We feel good and safe with our nurse and like her a lot. Sometimes we stop by her office just to chat.

If we don't feel well, our teacher gives us a pass to go see our nurse.

Mrs. Geary will examine us to find out what's wrong.

Ben might have a fever Can you please check his temp? Thank you! Nurse Pass 1/10/02 10:00

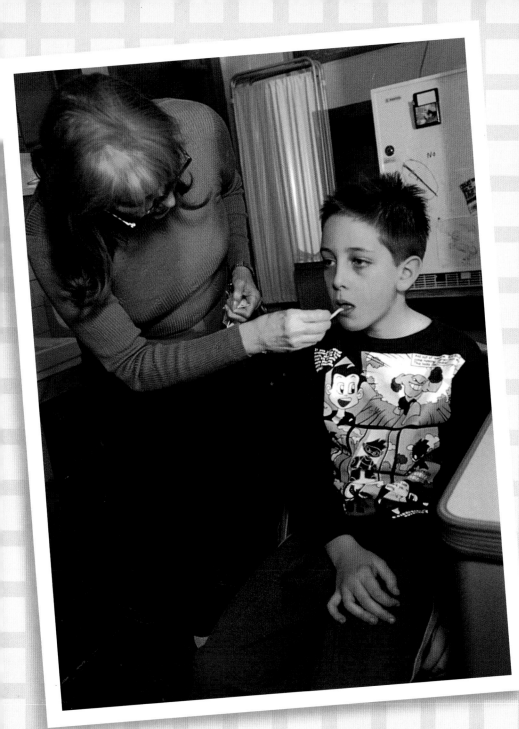

Often she checks our temperature with a thermometer to see if we have a fever.

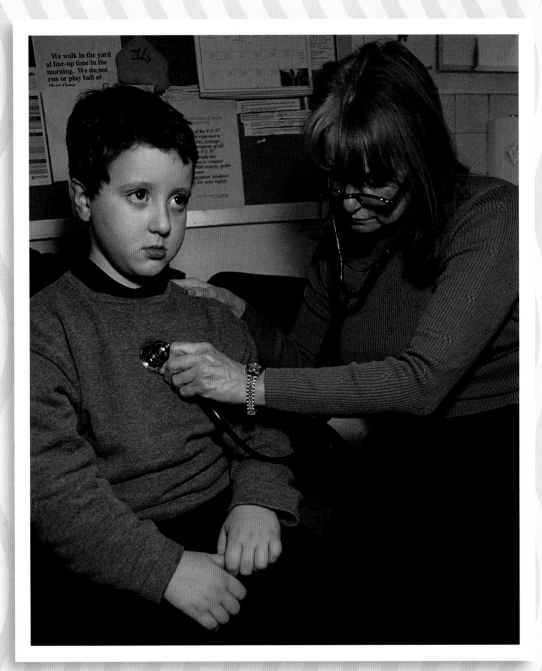

She also listens to our heart with her stethoscope. The stethoscope can tell her if our heart beats right and if it is strong.

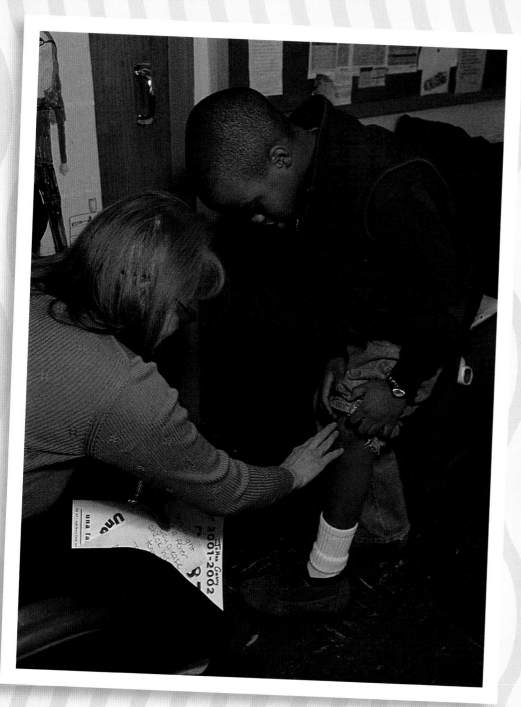

If we bump a knee or arm, Mrs. Geary puts ice on the place that is swollen. Ice makes bumps and bruises feel better and helps the swelling disappear.

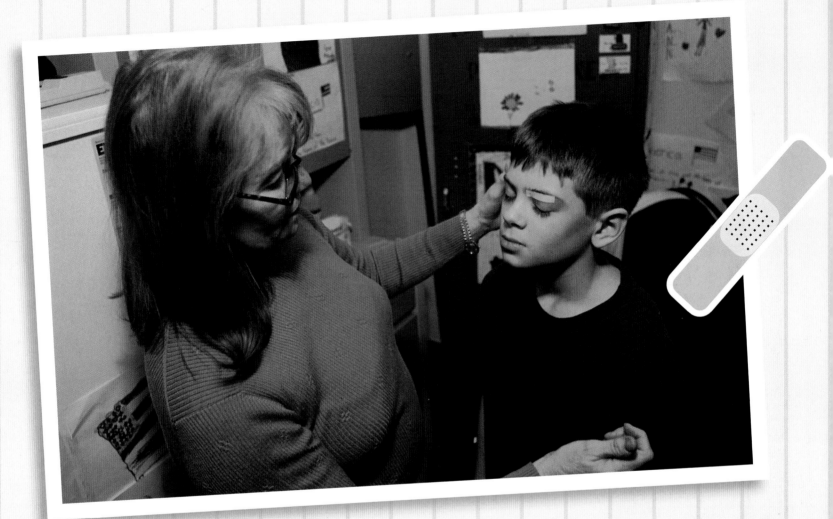

If we've cut ourselves, our nurse may cover our cut with a Band-Aid. Sometimes she puts medicine on it.

Mrs. Geary sometimes shows us how to wash our hands to get rid of germs. She explains that it is important to keep the area around a cut clean and not to touch the cut with dirty hands.

Our nurse has a couch in her office. When we feel sick, we can rest on the couch.

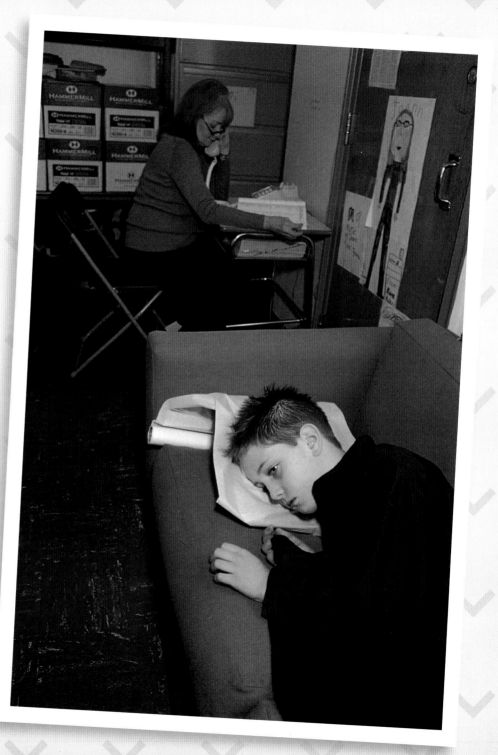

Then Mrs. Geary will call our parents and ask them to come get us.

We stay with Mrs. Geary until our parents can take us home.

There are times when some of us get bugs called lice in our hair. These bugs are not good for you, so every now and then Mrs. Geary checks our hair to make sure we don't have lice. If she finds any, she tells our parents. Then they can wash our hair with a special shampoo to get rid of the lice.

Some of us have to take
medicine during schooltime.
Our nurse makes sure we do.

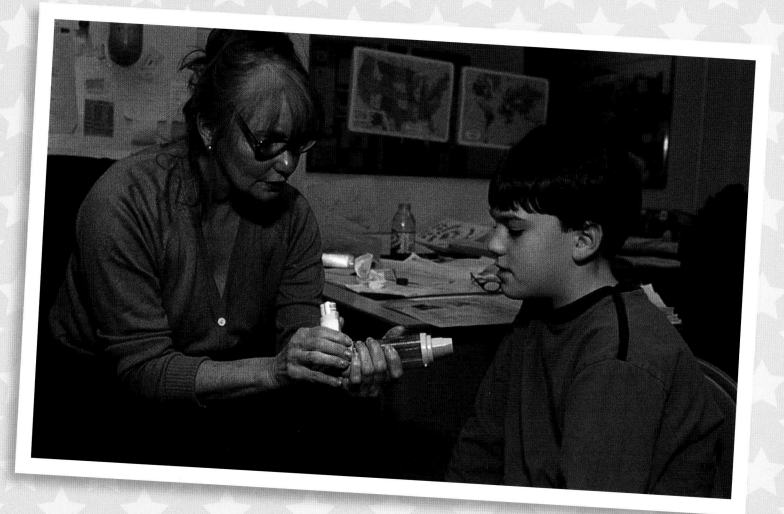

Some of us have asthma, a kind of breathing problem. If anyone has trouble breathing, Mrs. Geary has a special machine to make our breathing easier.

Mrs. Geary keeps records about everyone who visits her.

She marks a big chart to keep track of the children who are allergic to different foods and medicines.

Each time we visit her, she writes about
what is wrong in a special book called a log.

Sometimes Mrs. Geary meets with teachers and other people who work in our school. In certain cases she may discuss a child's illness with one of our teachers.

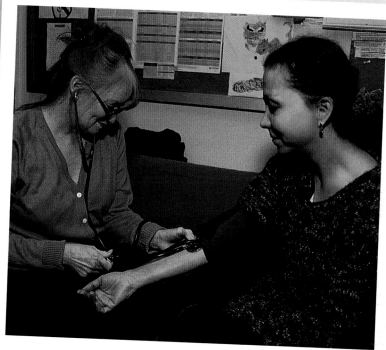

She may ask our school secretary to help keep the records and send notices to parents about their children's health.

If one of our teachers gets ill, she is there to help them, too.

Here (left) is our nurse as a child with her mother and her sister Margie.

Here is our nurse (seated with dark shirt) as a grown-up with all her sisters and her one brother.

Mrs. Geary has lived in Manhattan, a part of New York City, most of her life. She came from a large family of eight children—seven girls and one boy!

Her dad, a sports
writer, always said,
"My children
are my jewels!"
She was one
of his jewels!

Here is our nurse
with her father.

Now Mrs. Geary lives with her husband, Thornton, in an apartment house near the Hudson River. They like to spend time in the park—walking and talking and laughing together.

Sometimes Mrs. Geary buys flowers or fruit along the way. Mrs. Geary and her husband also enjoy reading together, visiting with friends and family, and playing with their kitten, Ebony.

When Mrs. Geary was young, she wanted to be a nurse because she liked helping people. At nursing school she was an excellent student and won several awards.

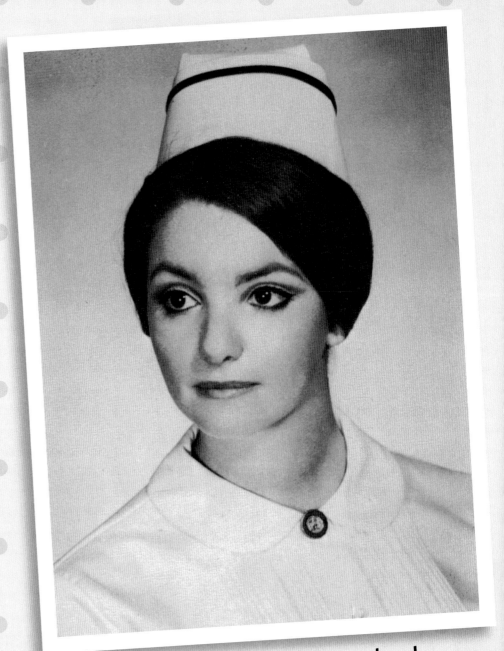

Our nurse in nursing school

Helping children get well is what she liked to do best—that is why she became a school nurse.

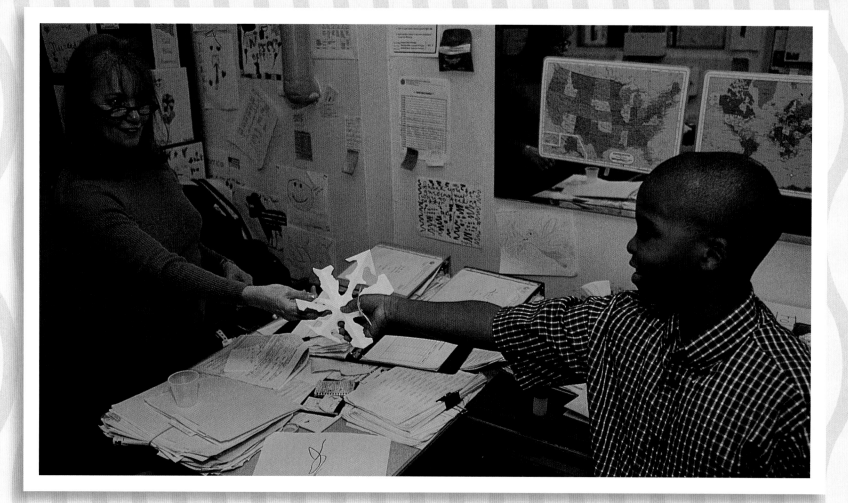

We're so glad we have
Mrs. Geary at our school.
SHE'S A GREAT NURSE!

THINGS TO DO

Would you like to
know more about
your nurse or
what it is like
to be a nurse?

Would you like
to do something nice
for your nurse?

Try one of these
activities.

Learn About Your Nurse

- Interview your school nurse. Find out all
  the things she or he does to help children
  at your school.

- Make a list of all the things the nurse has
  in her or his office. Draw a small picture
  next to each thing on the list.

- Invite your nurse to visit your class to talk
  with you about her or his work.

- Find out why students in your class visit
  the nurse.

Role Play

- In the dramatic play area of your classroom, set up a space where you can take care of sick dolls and animals.

- Be sure that you have all the supplies you need, such as a stethoscope, thermometer, bandages, a bed, and blankets. You can make many of these supplies yourself from old rags, cardboard, pieces of wood, glue, and plastic.

- You may want to bring old dolls and stuffed animals from home.

Make a Healthy Living Chart

Make a chart of things children can do to stay healthy. Draw a small picture next to each activity.

Learn These Words

asthma—a disease that makes it very hard to breathe

blood pressure—the force of your blood as it is carried away from your heart

fever—when your body's temperature gets higher than it should be

stethoscope—an instrument for listening to your heart

swollen—when a part of your body increases in size

thermometer—an instrument for measuring the temperature of your body

About the Author

Ann Morris loves children, and she loves writing books for children. She has written more than eighty books for children, including a series of books for The Millbrook Press about grandmothers and their grandchildren called *What Was It Like, Grandma?* For many years Ann Morris taught school. Eventually, she left teaching to become an editor with a children's book publishing company. While she still sometimes teaches workshops and seminars for teachers, Ann Morris now spends most of her time writing. She lives in New York City.

About the Photographer-Illustrator

Peter Linenthal is a talented photographer and illustrator. He studied fine arts at the San Francisco Art Institute. He is a native of California and teaches at the San Francisco Center for the Book. Peter Linenthal also loves children and working on books for children. He did the photographs and illustrations for Ann Morris's books about grandmothers.